NAPKIN FOLDING

FOR SPECIAL OCCASIONS

NAPKIN FOLDING

FOR SPECIAL OCCASIONS

Gay Merrill Gross

PHOTOGRAPHY BY BILL MILNE

MEREHURST

A FRIEDMAN GROUP BOOK

Published 1993 by Merehurst Limited
Ferry House, 51/57 Lacy Road
Putney, London, SW15 1PR

By arrangement with Michael Friedman Publishing Group, Inc.

Copyright © 1993 by Michael Friedman Publishing Group, Inc.

ISBN 1 85391 273 5

A catalogue record for this book is available from the British Library.

NAPKIN FOLDING FOR SPECIAL OCCASIONS
was prepared and produced by
Michael Friedman Publishing Group, Inc.
15 West 26th Street
New York, New York 10010

Editor: Sharyn Rosart
Art Direction/Designer: Devorah Levinrad
Photography Editor: Christopher C. Bain

Typeset by Classic Type, Inc.
Colour separations by Colourmatch Graphic Equipment & Services
Printed and bound in Hong Kong by Leefung-Asco Printers Ltd.

For my loving mother

Acknowledgments

Thank you to all who contributed creative ideas and assistance with the production of this book:

For creative ideas, Pearl Chin and Rachel Katz ❧ For contributing designs, Laura Kruskal, Ann Davenport, Jean Paul and Jacqueline Latil, Stephen Weiss, Beth Glogovcsan ❧ For research materials, Lillian Oppenheimer, Ruthanne Bessman, Ann Davenport, Mark Kennedy, Kathleen Beyer, John Cunliffe, Kathleen O'Regan, Anne Bedrick, Trish Troy Truitt, Bennett Arnstein, V'Ann Cornelius and the West Coast Origami Guild ❧ For proofreading, Tony Cheng and Jan Polish ❧ For the beautiful photographs, Bill Milne, photographer, and his assistant, Jim Columbo ❧ For the creative props and photo styling, the amazing Lynn McMahill and her assistant, Tori Shearer ❧ For their creative and artistic concepts, the talented staff at Michael Friedman Publishing Group: Sharyn Rosart, Editor; Devorah Levinrad, Book Designer; Jeff Batzli, Art Director; Christopher Bain, Photography Editor; Steven Arcella, Illustrator ❧ My own knowledge and education in the folding arts are enhanced by my many wonderful associations and friendships made through The Friends of The Origami Center of America. Thank you to Michael Shall, who founded this forum for folders, and to Lillian Oppenheimer, whose generous and sharing nature has laid the foundation for many organizations around the world devoted to the folding arts.

To the best of my knowledge, all designs used in this book are traditional unless otherwise credited.

Table of Contents

8   Introduction
10 Symbols Used in this Book
11 How to Fold a Napkin into Quarters

Holidays

14 New Year's Eve *Cocktail Coaster*
16 New Year's Day *Buffet Brunch Bundle*
18 Easter *Bunny*
21 Easter *Fleur-de-Lis*
24 Easter *Basket*
26 Easter *Twin Baskets*
29 Passover *Star of David*
32 Chanukah *Candle*
34 Christmas *Santa Claus*
37 Christmas *Elf's Boot*
40 Christmas *Christmas Tree*
42 Christmas *Standing Christmas Tree*
44 Christmas *Candy Cane*
46 Christmas *Stocking*

Seasonal Celebrations

50 First Day of Spring *Butterfly*
52 April Showers *Parasol*
54 May Day *Water Lily*
57 First Day of Summer *Yacht*
60 First Day of Summer *Shell*
62 Midsummer *Ice Cream Cone*
64 Summer Picnic *Picnic Package*
66 First Day of Autumn *Double Leaf*
68 First Day of Autumn *Happi Coat*
70 Autumn Harvest Moon *Fireside Flame*
72 First Day of Winter *Icicle*
74 First Snowfall *Snowflake*
76 Midwinter *Sleigh*

Birthdays

80 Mother's Birthday *Rose*
83 Mother's Birthday *Corsage*
86 Father's Birthday *Necktie*
88 Father's Birthday *Shirt*
90 Grandmother's Birthday *Orchid*
92 Grandfather's Birthday *Bowtie*
94 Child's Birthday *Pinwheel*
96 Child's Birthday *Clown's Hat*
98 Baby's Birthday *Diaper*

Romantic Occasions

102 Dinner for Two *Valentine Heart*
104 Dinner for Two *Lover's Knot*
106 Anniversary *Sweetheart*
108 Wedding *Layered Heart*
110 Breakfast in Bed *Triple Tier*

Parties

114 Formal Dinner Party *Double Fan*
116 Formal Dinner Party *Wave*
118 Garden Party *Tulip*
120 Tea Party *Lazy Susan*
122 Children's Party *Cat's Ears*
124 Children's Party *Surprise Sack*

126 Picture Index

Introduction

For holidays and occasions when you want everything to be festive and special, nothing is simpler or more effective than dressing up your table with decoratively folded napkin designs. Napkins provide the perfect way to create a mood, establish a theme, add a splash of color, and coordinate your table setting.

Napkin designs can also provide an outlet for your own creativity. You can follow the suggestions for each holiday or mix and match designs and occasions. For instance, a Winter Snowflake folded from bright colors can become a New Year's Fireworks Starburst. Fold the Candy Cane from pastel colors and it becomes a May Day Maypole.

Experiment with different patterns, colors, and textures in napkins. Look for interesting ribbons and accessories to use with the folds. Real flowers, dried flowers, and other flora can add seasonal charm to the napkin design.

You can also vary the folding patterns of the designs themselves. Add extra pleats, pull the free point down, stagger the overlapping layers—see what new variations you can create. Or start from scratch and try folding the napkin in different ways. Many of the designs in this book are derived from origami (folded paper) designs. Try out techniques you may use in sewing, or draping a scarf to enhance an outfit; they may work to add distinction to your table!

Here are some general guidelines to keep in mind when folding napkins:

- *Unless otherwise specified, most napkin designs can be folded from either cloth or paper napkins. Experiment ahead of time to see which types and sizes of napkins work best for a particular design.*

- *When buying new paper or cloth napkins, be aware that most napkin designs require a perfectly square napkin. If you cannot find square paper napkins, trim off the longer side with scissors.*

- *When shopping for cloth napkins, look for linen, all-cotton, or cotton-polyester blends. Avoid all-polyester napkins as these will not hold a crease well.*

- *For the best results, iron out all the creases in a cloth napkin before you begin folding. If the creases in a paper napkin conflict with the design, press them out with a finger or an iron set at a low temperature setting.*

- *If you are having trouble keeping the folds in place, try using a little spray starch when you iron the napkins. Or, you may need to use a different type of napkin.*

- *Always fold on a clean, flat surface such as the dining room table.*

- *If your napkin is patterned on one side only, it is obvious which is the better side of the napkin. Otherwise, look at the hem of your napkin to determine which is the better side. When following the folding instructions you will generally begin with the better or patterned side of the napkin facing down, unless the instructions tell you to do otherwise.*

- *Napkins can be folded early in the day, or even the day before a party, and set aside.*

- *Read through the "Symbols Used In This Book" section at the beginning of this book. It will help you in following the step-by-step drawings.*

- *When following the diagrams, if a step is unclear, look ahead to the next drawing and see what the result of the step should look like.*

Decoratively folded napkins can also be used to create a centerpiece. Here are some suggestions:

- *Place several Candy Cane napkins into a wicker basket with some pine cones and let them point out of the basket like a starburst.*

- *Stand the Candle napkins in a row to create a candelabra effect.*

Whether the calendar says it's a holiday or you decide to make any day a special occasion, decorating with napkins is fun to do and offers your guests a warm welcome to the table.

Symbols Used In This Book

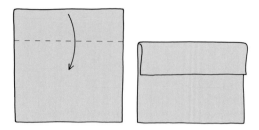

A line of dashes means to fold forward or toward yourself.

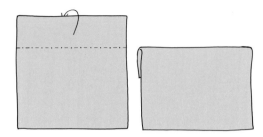

A line of alternating dashes and dots means to fold backward or away from yourself.

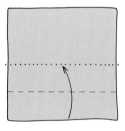

A dotted line indicates a hidden or imaginary line used as a reference mark.

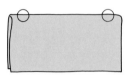

A circle means to hold the napkin here.

An arrow with multiple loops means to roll the napkin in the direction of the arrow.

A looped arrow means to turn the napkin over in the direction of the arrow.

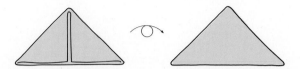

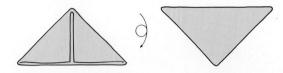

From left to right   From top to bottom

How to Fold a Napkin in Quarters

Some of the directions in this book instruct you to begin with a napkin folded into quarters. If you are using a paper napkin, it is probably already folded into quarters in the package and you are ready to begin. If you are using a cloth napkin, here are instructions for folding an open napkin into quarters:

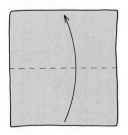

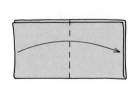

four free corners

1. Fold the napkin in half.   2. Fold in half again.   3. Your napkin is now folded into quarters. One corner will have four free corners. The beginning instruction for the fold will usually tell you where to place this corner.

Holidays

NEW YEAR'S EVE
Cocktail Coaster

Party guests can use this versatile fold as a coaster before dinner and then unfold it when the meal is served.

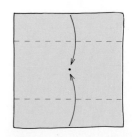

1. Begin with an open napkin. Fold the top and bottom edges inward to meet at the center.

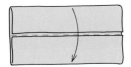

2. Bring the top edge down to the bottom edge, folding the napkin in half.

3. Imagine an invisible line at the horizontal center of the napkin. Fold the bottom left corner up to this line, forming a sharp angle at the top left corner.

4. Bring the folded edge created in step 3 down so that it lies directly over the long bottom edge.

5. You have created an equilateral triangle at the left side of your napkin. Bring the left edge up to lie directly over the long top edge.

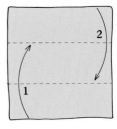

6. Continue in this manner, adding two more layers to your equilateral triangle.

7. a) Fold down a small triangle at the top right corner. b) Tuck the bottom right corner into the pocket formed by the layers of the large triangle.

8. The finished Cocktail Coaster.

Variation: For a larger Coaster, begin by folding the napkin in thirds, then continue from step 3. Omit step 6.

NEW YEAR'S DAY

NEW YEAR'S DAY
Buffet Brunch Bundle

Your guests will appreciate the convenience of having their silverware and napkin wrapped togther in this decorative and practical Buffet Bundle.

1. Begin with a square napkin folded into quarters. Place the silverware in the center of the napkin as shown in the drawing. Fold a small triangle in on each side corner.

2. Fold the napkin in thirds, enclosing the silverware in the napkin.

3. Tie a ribbon around the package.

4. The Bundle is ready for your buffet table.

E A S T E R

Bunny

This delightful fold requires a large, lightweight napkin. If you are using a 3-ply paper napkin, separate the layers and fold the Bunny from only a single or double layer.

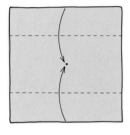

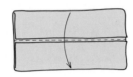

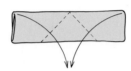

1. Begin with an open napkin. Fold the top and bottom edges inward to meet at the center.

2. Bring the top edge down to the bottom edge, folding the napkin in half.

3. Place a finger at the center of the top edge and fold each half of the long top edge down so that they meet at the center.

4. Fold the right and left bottom edges up to the center.

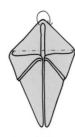

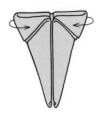

5. Narrow each bottom point by folding the outside edge to the center.

6. Fold the top point backward along the horizontal folded edges.

7. Bring the top side points toward each other…

8. …and lock one into the triangular pocket of the other.

Bunny

 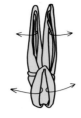 

9. Insert a finger inside the top of the napkin and give it a round shape. Holding onto the lock, flip the napkin over from top to bottom.

10. Open out and shape the face and ears.

11. Finished Bunny.

EASTER

Fleur-de-Lis

This popular, traditional design gives a stately look to any table setting.

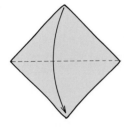

1. Begin with a square, open napkin, with one corner pointing toward you. Bring the top corner down to the bottom corner, forming a triangle.

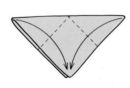

2. Place a finger at the center of the long folded edge and bring the right and left side points down to the bottom corner.

3. Fold the top point down so that it lies approximately 2 inches (5 cm) above the bottom points.

4. Take the point you folded down in step 3, and fold it up to the top edge.

5. Holding the napkin securely at the top, turn it over from top to bottom.

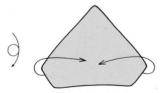

6. Bring the right and left side corners toward each other…

7. …and tuck the right corner into the pocket on the left.

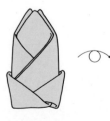

8. Holding the locked corners securely in place, round out the bottom of the napkin design, turn the napkin over, and stand it up.

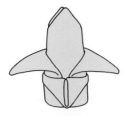

9. Leave the napkin as is for a Bishop's Hat, or…

10. …pull the top points out to the sides for the Fleur-de-Lis.

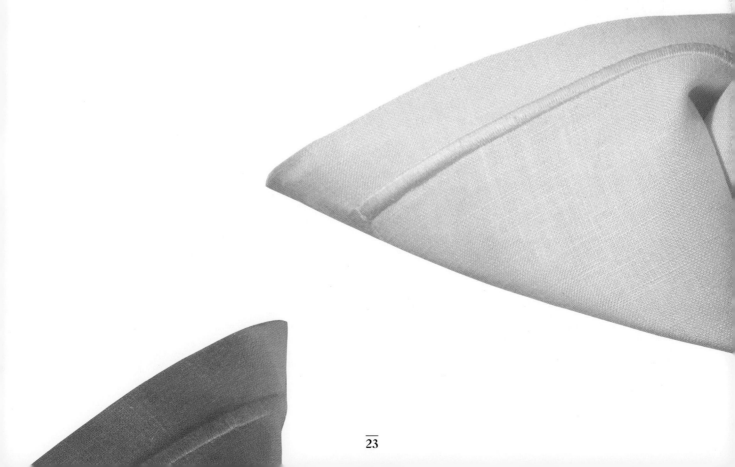

E A S T E R
Basket

Adorn your Easter table with this easy-to-make Basket. This fold requires a stiff napkin that will hold its shape.

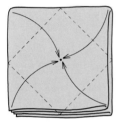

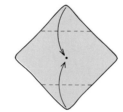

1. Begin with a square napkin folded into quarters. Place the four free corners at the bottom left and the double corner at the bottom right. Fold the four outside corners to the center.

2. Carefully flip the napkin over from bottom to top.

3. Fold the top and bottom corners inward to meet at the center.

4. Carefully flip the napkin over from top to bottom.

5. Keeping the bottom of the napkin flat on the table, gently push inward at the side points. The upper layers of the napkin will rise up at a right angle to the base of the napkin, forming a 3-dimensional container.

6. Shape the Basket by pinching the corners and add a ribbon handle if you wish.

Variation: To make a deeper basket, fold the top and bottom corners inward in step 3, but do not bring them all the way to the center. Then continue with step 4 as before.

E A S T E R
Twin Baskets

Here's a clever design that forms two compartments, perfect for holding Easter eggs or candy. Use a large, cotton napkin (at least 20" [51 cm] square).

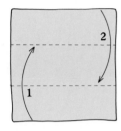

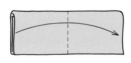

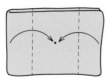

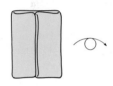

1. Begin with an open napkin. Fold the napkin in thirds, as you would fold a letter.

2. Bring the left side over to the right side, folding the napkin in half.

3. Fold the right and left sides inward to meet at the center.

4. Turn the napkin over from side to side.

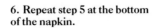

5. Push both top corners inside, forming a new inner layer and a point at the center of the top edge with two smaller points behind it (see drawing at step 6).

6. Repeat step 5 at the bottom of the napkin.

7. Grasp the top point (leaving the smaller points in place) and bring it down to form a diamond shape.

8. Grasp the bottom point and fold it up, forming a second diamond that overlaps the first.

9. Bring the right and left sides of the napkin together, folding it in half.

10. Turn the napkin over, stand it on the table, and open the Twin Baskets.

PASSOVER
Star of David

(Adapted by Beth Glogovcsan)

This design is based on an origami technique for folding a square into an equilateral triangle and a traditional European folding pattern for making the star. It relies on creases made in the napkin that serve as landmarks for the creases that follow. Try it first with a crisp paper napkin that will show a strong crease. When you are familiar with the design you can try it with a starched cloth napkin (iron the creases in place, if necessary). This design is more challenging than most napkin folds, so have patience if you are making it for the first time.

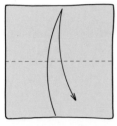

1. Begin with an open, square napkin. Fold the napkin in half, make a sharp crease, and unfold.

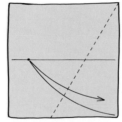

2. This next fold originates at the top right corner. It is formed by bringing the bottom right corner to touch the horizontal centerline. Make a sharp crease and unfold.

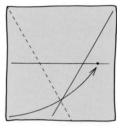

3. Repeat step 2 on the left side. Leave this fold in place.

4. Find the small crease line near the bottom of the napkin. The spot where this crease meets the long folded edge is the guide for this step. Fold the bottom edge of the napkin up, beginning at this guide mark.

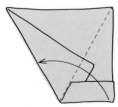

5. Refold on the crease made in step 2.

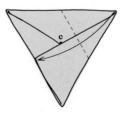

6. For future reference, note the location of centerpoint C. Then fold the top right point down to the center of the opposite edge.

7. Fold the same point back up again, making a new fold right over centerpoint C.

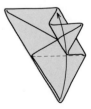

8. Fold the bottom point up to the right corner of the top edge.

9. Fold the same point back down again, creating a new crease over centerpoint C.

10. Fold the top left point down to the opposite point.

11. Fold the same point out again, creating a new crease over centerpoint C.

12. Optional Lock: Lift corner A for a moment and tuck it under the the layer of napkin beneath it.

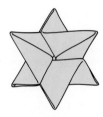

13. Turn the napkin over.

14. Finished Star of David.

CHANUKAH
Candle

Each of the eight days of Chanukah is marked by the lighting of candles.
This Candle napkin design is a nice way to reflect the "Festival of Lights"
theme at your holiday table.

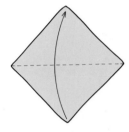

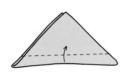

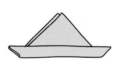

1. Begin with an open, square napkin, with one corner pointing toward you. Bring the bottom corner up to the top corner, forming a triangle.

2. Fold the bottom edge up, forming a hem approximately 2 inches (5 cm) wide.

3. Holding the hem tightly to keep it in place, carefully turn the napkin over, and rotate it so that the long folded edge is at the right.

4. Roll up the long right edge of the napkin from bottom to top. Stop rolling before you reach the very end, leaving a small tail at the top.

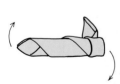

5. Rotate the napkin so that the cylinder is now standing up, with the band at the bottom.

6. Neatly tuck the small tail into the band, locking the loose end in place.

7. At the top of the roll are two loose points. Bend the first point backward and tuck it inside the roll. Shape the second point to resemble a candle flame.

8. Your completed Candle can stand or lie on the table next to each place setting.

CHRISTMAS
Santa Claus

(Design by the author)

For this fun design you will need two square paper napkins, one red and one white.
Each napkin should be 13 inches (33 cm) square or smaller.

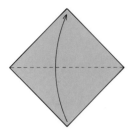 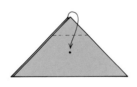 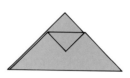 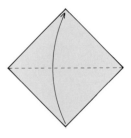

1. Begin with an open, square, red napkin, with one corner pointing toward you. Bring the bottom corner up to the top corner, forming a triangle.

2. At the top of the triangle are two loose corners. Take the first corner only and fold it down approximately one-third the height of the triangle.

3. Repeat step 1 with the white napkin.

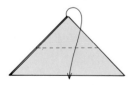 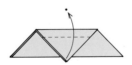 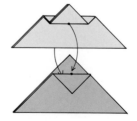 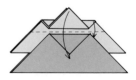

4. Fold the top corners of the white napkin down to a little past the bottom edge.

5. Take the same corners and fold them back up, creating a new crease approximately ¾ inch (2 cm) below the top edge.

6. Insert the white napkin behind the short folded edge of the red napkin. Position the two napkins so that the folded edges of each are just touching.

7. Flip the white napkin down along the line where the red and white napkins meet. (Be sure to include the horizontal band behind the white triangle.)

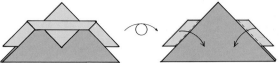 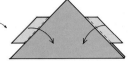  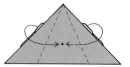

8. Check to be sure the bottom point of the white triangle is at the vertical center of the red napkin. Carefully turn the napkins over from side to side.

9. Fold the right and left short white tabs over the edges of the large red triangle.

10. Tuck the white tabs under the red triangle.

11. Fold the long slanted sides of the triangle inward to meet at the center.

12. Turn the napkin over from side to side.

13. Finished Santa Claus.

CHRISTMAS
Elf's Boot

Amuse your guests with this cute Boot fold. Use a cloth or a large paper napkin.

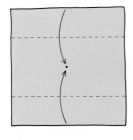

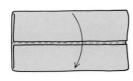

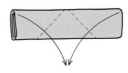

1. Begin with an open napkin. Fold the top and bottom edges inward to meet at the center.

2. Fold the top edge down to the bottom edge, folding the napkin in half.

3. Place a finger at the center of the long top edge and fold each half of that edge down to almost meet at the center (leave a small gap).

4. Fold the slanted right and left edges inward toward the center.

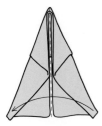

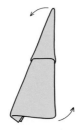

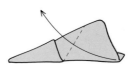

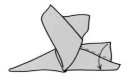

5. Fold the right half over the left half as if you were closing a book.

6. Rotate the napkin so that the sharp top point is at the left.

7. There are two tails on the right. Fold the top tail up as shown.

8. Narrow the lower tail by folding the top edge down to the bottom.

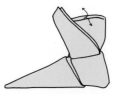

9. Bring the narrowed tail over toward the left and tuck it inside the toe pocket until it is secure.

10. Separate one of the loose layers at the top of the boot and pull it away from the other layers to give the boot leg a rounded top.

11. Completed Boot. If you wish, give it a turned-up toe.

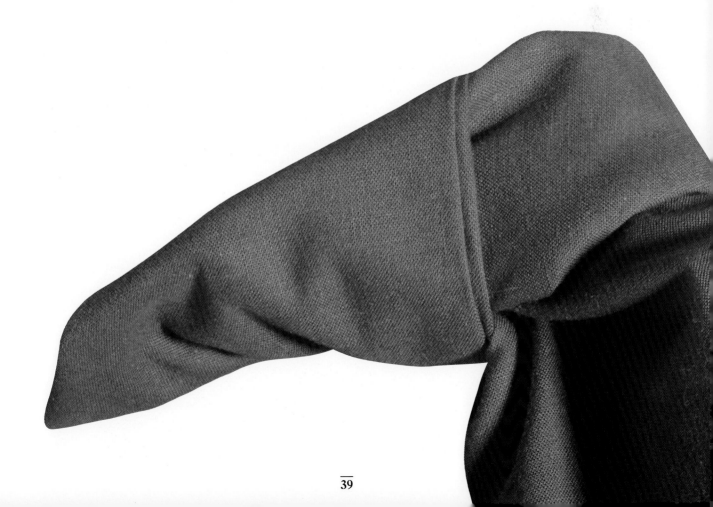

CHRISTMAS
Christmas Tree

*The Christmas Tree requires a napkin that will hold a crease well. Use a square
paper napkin or square cotton napkin, ironing the creases in place, if necessary.*

 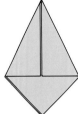 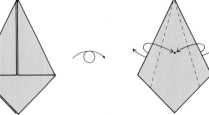 

1. Begin with a square napkin, folded into quarters. The four free corners are at the bottom pointing toward you. Fold the right and left top edges inward, to meet at the center.

2. Turn the napkin over from side to side.

3. Fold the long sides inward to meet at the center. As you do so, allow the underneath edges to swing out to the sides.

4. Fold the bottom point backward, slightly below the spot where the folded edges meet at the center.

5. Finished Christmas Tree.

CHRISTMAS

Standing Christmas Tree

Add festivity to this design by putting a commercial or handmade star atop each napkin tree.

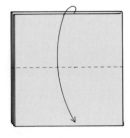

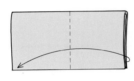

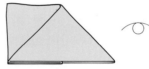

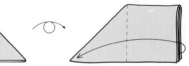

1. Begin with a square napkin folded into quarters. The four free corners are at the bottom left. Fold the napkin in half, from top to bottom.

2. Place a finger at the center of the top edge. With your other hand, pick up the first corner at the bottom right. Bring this corner to lie over the bottom left corners.

3. Turn the napkin over from left to right.

4. Place a finger at the left corner of the top edge of the napkin. Lift up, as a group, the first four corners at the bottom right. Bring them to lie over the bottom left point.

5. Fold the napkin in half.

6. Stand the napkin up and slightly separate the four "branches." If you wish, add a star to your finished Standing Christmas Tree.

CHRISTMAS
Candy Cane

*Create a wonderful holiday effect with this simple-to-make design. Use two cloth or
paper napkins of equal size, but different colors.*

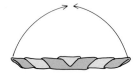

1. Place one open napkin over the other. The top napkin should be slightly higher, creating a V-shaped border approximately 1 inch (2.5 cm) wide.

2. Starting at the bottom corner, roll both napkins together toward the top corner.

3. Bring the right and left ends of the roll together, loosely folding the roll in half.

4. The finished Candy Cane can be draped across a plate or inserted into a glass.

CHRISTMAS
Stocking

This Christmas Stocking can be folded from a paper or small cloth napkin. If you use paper, try folding two different colored napkins together as one. This will create a different colored cuff at the top of the Stocking. Insert a candy cane or other Christmas candy so that it peeks out the top of the Stocking. You can also insert a name card into the pocket.

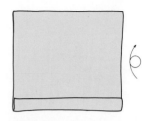

1. Begin with an open napkin. The better, or patterned, side should be facing up. Fold the bottom edge up to form a hem approximately 1½ inches (4 cm) wide.

2. Holding the hem in place, turn the napkin over from bottom to top.

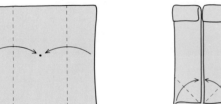

3. The hem should now be at the back of the top edge. Fold the right and left sides inward to meet at the center.

4. Fold the bottom corners up to meet at the vertical center.

5. Fold the bottom point up to meet the corners you folded up in step 4.

6. Fold the short bottom edge of the napkin up to the top of the napkin.

7. Fold the short edge back down again, creating a new fold approximately one-quarter the distance up from the bottom to the top edge.

8. Bring the right side of the napkin over to the left, folding the napkin in half.

9. Hold the left edge of the napkin just above the pleat formed in step 7. Hold the bottom edge in your other hand and very gently pull it to the right, forming the foot end of the Stocking, as shown in the next drawing.

10. Completed Stocking. If you folded it from paper, write each guest's name across the cuff at the top.

Seasonal
Celebrations

FIRST DAY OF SPRING

Butterfly

*The Butterfly is a beautiful but challenging design.
Try it when you feel comfortable with easier folds. Use
a paper or large cloth napkin that will hold a crease.
The patterned, or good, side of the napkin
should be facing down.*

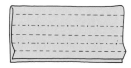

1. Fold the napkin in half from top to bottom. Then grasp the bottom edge of the top layer only and accordion-pleat the napkin up to the top folded edge.

2. Holding the pleats in place, carefully flip the napkin over from top to bottom.

3. Place a finger at the center of the bottom edge. Bring the bottom right corner (and the pleated layers behind it) up to the center of the top edge. Repeat with the bottom left corner.

4. Being careful not to disturb the pleats, carefully flip the napkin over from top to bottom.

5. Bring the bottom corners up and tuck them under the triangular pocket at the top.

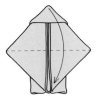

6. Bring the top corner down to the bottom of the napkin.

7. Bring the same corner back up again so that it extends a little beyond the top edge, as shown in the next drawing.

8. Bring the side points towards each other and insert one inside the other, as shown in the next drawing.

9. Turn the napkin over from side to side, being careful not to disturb the points you have just locked.

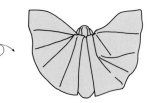

10. Spread the pleats and shape the body for your finished Butterfly.

APRIL SHOWERS
Parasol

Choose a lovely print for this charming springtime design. To help in holding the pleats together as you tie a ribbon around them, temporarily slip the closed end through a napkin ring and tie the ribbon above the ring so it can easily be slipped off again.

  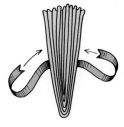 

1. Start with an open napkin. Beginning at the bottom edge, accordion-pleat the napkin up to the top edge.

2. Hold the ends of the pleats firmly in each hand. Bring both ends together, folding the pile of pleats in half.

3. Tie a ribbon around the middle of the pleats or insert them into a napkin ring.

4. Fan out the pleats for your finished Parasol.

M A Y D A Y
Water Lily

The Water Lily is a beautiful napkin fold. It will add a decorative touch to any table it adorns. Practice this fold ahead of time so you can learn the technique for forming the petals. Use a square cotton, linen, or paper napkin.

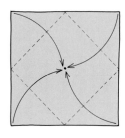

1. Begin with an open, square napkin. Fold all four corners inward to meet at the center.

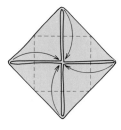

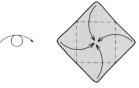

2. Fold the four new outside corners inward to meet at the center.

3. Again, fold the four new outside corners inward to meet at the center.

4. Holding the four flaps securely in place, carefully turn the napkin over.

5. Fold the four corners inward to meet at the center.

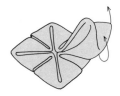

6. It is crucial that you hold the four loose points at the center securely in place during the next steps. Use your fingers, or place a glass on top of them. Bend one corner toward the center until a point from the underneath layer is set free.

7. Grasp the freed point and gently tug it upwards until it softly wraps around the other point like a high-backed collar.

8. Continue steps 6 and 7 on all four corners of the napkin. This forms the inner layer of petals on your Water Lily.

9. Reach between two petals to the underneath layers of the napkin. When you feel the corner of a flap, pull it out and gently tug it upward. Repeat three more times. This will form the second layer of petals.

10. Reach behind each petal from the first layer to find the last layer of petals. Gently pull each one out from underneath the flower and tug it gently upward.

11. The completed Water Lily. It can stand alone or its cuplike shape makes it a suitable container.

Variation: If you are using a small paper napkin or a small, stiff cloth napkin, omit steps 3 and 10. Your Water Lily will have eight petals instead of twelve.

FIRST DAY OF SUMMER
Yacht

(Design by Ann Davenport)

Anchors aweigh! This napkin fold will surely put you in the spirit for a sail.

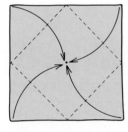

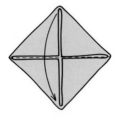

1. Begin with an open, square napkin. Fold the four corners to the center.

2. Bring the top point down to the bottom point, being careful not to disturb the layers you folded in at step 1.

3. Fold the napkin in half from left to right.

4. Rotate the napkin slightly so that the long edge of the triangle is at the bottom.

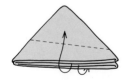

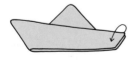

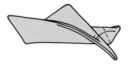

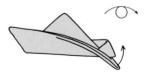

5. You should have four folded edges at the bottom. Separate them—two in one hand, two in the other hand—and turn them up in front and in back, as if turning up the cuff on a sleeve.

6. Adjust the size of the cuff to give the boat the shape you would like. There are two loose points on the right. Pull the first one slightly down and…

7. …tuck the second point over the folded edge.

8. Replace the first point to its original position and turn the napkin over from right to left.

9. The loose point is now at the left side of the boat. Pull it slightly up and tuck it into the layers that form the hull of the boat.

10. Stand up your finished Yacht.

FIRST DAY OF SUMMER
Shell

(Design by the author)

The Shell brings the seaside to your table.

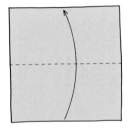

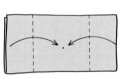

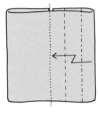

1. Begin with an open napkin. Bring the bottom edge up to the top edge, folding the napkin in half.

2. Fold the right and left sides inward to meet at the center.

3. Flip the napkin over from bottom to top.

4. Accordion-pleat one half of the napkin into thirds.

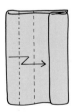

5. Accordion-pleat the other half of the napkin into thirds.

6. Carefully fold the bottom half of the napkin backward so that the bottom edges lie behind the top edges.

7. Gently pull the two loose corners on the near and far layers at the top right corner of the napkin. The napkin should spread out at the top only. Repeat on the left side.

8. Finished Shell.

MIDSUMMER
Ice Cream Cone

(Collected by Jacqueline and Jean Paul Latil)

The front of this design has three deep pockets for silverware, chopsticks, breadsticks, or a flower. For a secret message or surprise, use the hidden pocket on the back.

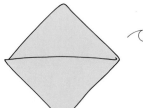

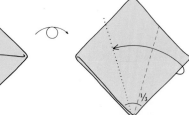

1. Begin with a napkin folded into quarters. Place the four free corners at the left, with the double corner at the top. Separate the two flaps at the top and fold the first layer down to the bottom corner.

2. Turn the napkin over from left to right.

3. Fold the bottom right edges over to the left, creating a sharp point at the bottom corner.

4. Notice the folded edge marked A. Fold the bottom left edges over to the right. (You should now have divided the bottom corner into even thirds.) Adjust the folds if necessary.

5. Fold corner B backward, tucking it behind folded edge A.

6. Completed Ice Cream Cone.

SUMMER PICNIC
Picnic Package

When dining outdoors, give each picnic-goer this handy fold. It wraps up the necessary silverware and two napkins into one neat little package. When unfolded, the second napkin can be used as a placemat.

Use two large napkins in contrasting colors.

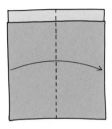

1. Place one open napkin over the other so that the top edges are approximately 2 inches (5 cm) apart. Fold the napkins in half, bringing the left side over to the right side.

2. Place the silverware in the middle of the napkin, then bring the sides in, folding the napkin approximately in thirds so that the silverware is covered.

3. Fold the bottom edge up as far as the silverware inside will allow.

4. Fold the top edge down, tucking it inside the layers folded up from the bottom.

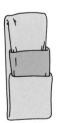

5. Finished Picnic Package.

FIRST DAY OF AUTUMN

FIRST DAY OF AUTUMN
Double Leaf

This fold will look especially dramatic if made from two napkins folded together. Because of the extra thickness, instead of a napkin ring, use ribbon, jute twine, or raffia to hold the pleats together.

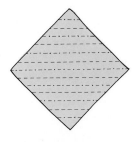

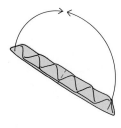

1. Begin with an open napkin. Accordion-pleat the napkin from the bottom corner up to the top corner.

2. With one hand, hold the pleats in place at the center of the napkin. With your other hand, bring the right and left sides up to the top.

3. Slide the bottom of the napkin through a napkin ring.

4. Fan out the pleats for your finished Double Leaf.

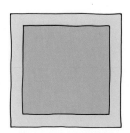

Variation: a) Use two napkins of different sizes and colors placed as shown, and fold them together as one.

Variation: b) Make the fold in step 2 off-center to create a large leaf and a small leaf.

FIRST DAY OF AUTUMN
Happi Coat

As the weather gets chillier, this Japanese-style jacket will add a stylish touch to your table. Begin with a napkin folded in half from top to bottom.

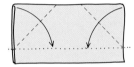

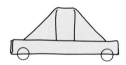

1. Imagine an invisible horizontal line, approximately 1¾ inches (4.5 cm) above the bottom edges of the napkin. Bring the top right and left corners to this invisible line, forming equal-sized triangles (see next drawing).

2. Fold the bottom edges up, forming a hem that lies over the triangles.

3. Hold the napkin securely at the sides and turn it over from bottom to top.

4. Place a finger at the center of the top edge. Fold the right and left sides down so that they meet at the center.

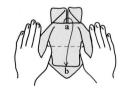

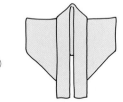

5. Flip the napkin over from top to bottom.

6. Find the right and left triangular pockets. Insert a thumb in each pocket and gently pull your hands apart. As you do so, edge A will lift up and almost touch edge B.

7. Notice that your triangular pockets have disappeared and have been replaced by one rectangular shape. Carefully hold the napkin and turn it over from bottom to top.

8. Finished Happi Coat.

AUTUMN HARVEST MOON
Fireside Flame

Bring the warmth of a fireplace to your table with this fairly simple design. You will need two paper napkins or two lightweight cloth napkins.

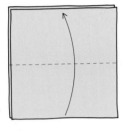

1. Begin with two open napkins. Place one napkin directly over the other and fold them together as one. Bring both bottom edges up to meet the top edges.

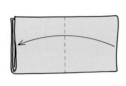

2. Fold the right edges over to meet the left edges.

3. Slightly rotate the napkins so that the eight free corners are at the top.

4. Fold the bottom corner up approximately one-third the height of the diamond shape.

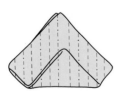

5. Accordion-pleat the napkins from one side corner to the other.

6. Insert the bottom of the napkins into a glass. Separate all eight layers at the top of the napkin.

7. Gently shape the layers of the napkin for your completed Fireside Flame.

Variation: You may also fold this design from a single napkin for a more delicate, flower-like look.

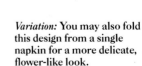

FIRST DAY OF WINTER
Icicle

(Design by Laura Kruskal)

Its graceful shape makes this a very elegant fold.

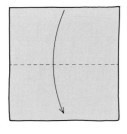

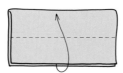

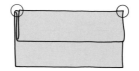

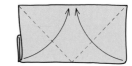

1. Begin with an open napkin. The patterned, or better, side of the napkin should be facing up. Bring the top edge down to the bottom edge.

2. Bring the bottom edge of the first layer only up to the top edge.

3. Hold the napkin at the top corners and flip it over from top to bottom.

4. Place a finger at the center of the bottom edge, and fold the bottom corners (all layers) up to the center of the top edge.

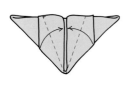

5. Fold the slanted side edges inward to meet at the center.

6. The Icicle design is complete. If you wish, insert silverware or chopsticks into the two pockets.

FIRST SNOWFALL
Snowflake

(Adapted by the author)

Dress up your table with winter's jewel—the Snowflake.

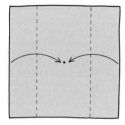

1. Begin with an open napkin. The better side should be facing up. Fold the sides inward to meet at the center.

2. Turn the napkin over.

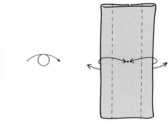

3. As you fold the side edges inward to the center, allow the underneath edges to flip out to the sides.

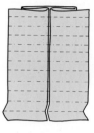

4. Carefully accordion-pleat the napkin from bottom to top.

5. Hold the pleats in place as you tie a narrow ribbon around the center.

6. Fan the pleats out to form a full circle for your completed Snowflake.

MIDWINTER
Sleigh

On a wintery day, cheer up your guests with this napkin Sleigh! Use a cotton napkin.

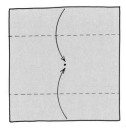

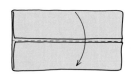

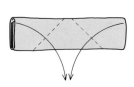

1. Begin with an open napkin. Fold the top and bottom edges inward to meet at the center.

2. Fold the top edge down to the bottom edge.

3. Leaving a small gap in the center, fold each side of the top edge down toward the center.

4. Roll each short end up until you can just see the edges underneath.

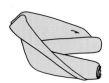

5. Holding the rolls tightly in place with one hand, fold the top point backward a little to blunt the tip.

6. Still holding onto the rolls, fold the napkin in half and place it on a plate, so that it is standing on the rolls. Your Sleigh is complete.

Birthdays

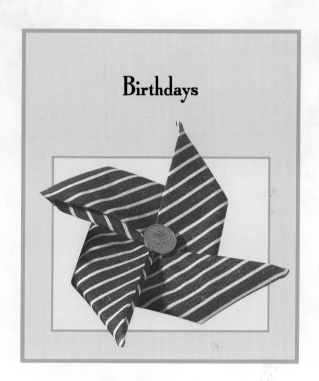

MOTHER'S BIRTHDAY

MOTHER'S BIRTHDAY

Rose

(Collected by Stephen Weiss)

*Fold this popular flower from a large paper napkin. As an added touch, spray a little
cologne on each paper flower.*

   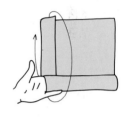

1. Begin with an open, paper napkin. If the napkin is 3-ply, separate the layers and fold a Rose from each. At the left edge, fold over a hem approximately 2½ inches (7 cm) wide.

2. Curl up the bottom edge of the napkin and wrap the hem edge once around the index finger of your left hand. Hold it in place with the middle finger.

3. Grasp the left side of the top edge of the napkin and bring it down and up, winding the hem end around three fingers.

4. Bring the top edge down and up again, winding the hem end around four fingers.

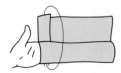 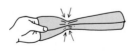 

5. If the hem end is not yet completely wound around the four fingers of your left hand, continue winding it loosely until the napkin is completely rolled up.

6. With your right hand, tightly pinch the napkin at the ends of your left fingers. Holding the pinch firmly, remove your left hand.

7. With both hands, continue to pinch the napkin at the base of the flower, then begin twisting a stem under the flower by tightly pinching the napkin and twisting your hands in opposite directions. Helpful hint for making a successful stem: Pinch and twist as tightly as you can, without tearing the napkin.

8. Continue twisting until you reach one-third down the length of the stem. Find the loose outside corner at the bottom of the stem end. Gently pull at this corner and lift it up until the tip of the corner reaches the flower. This will form the rose's leaf.

9. Tightly pinch the base of the leaf and continue twisting until you reach the bottom of the stem.

10. Finished Rose. Fold several for a bouquet.

MOTHER'S BIRTHDAY

Corsage

This pretty flower is best made from a small paper napkin approximately 13 inches (33 cm) square. A stiff cotton napkin, approximately 15 inches (38 cm) square can also be used.

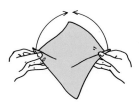

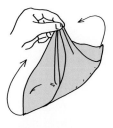

1. Begin with an open, square napkin, with one corner pointing toward you. Pinch the right and left side corners of the napkin so that the center of the pinch points up.

Bring your hands together, until the folded edges of the two pinched corners just touch each other.

2. Hold the pinched corners together in one hand. With your other hand, bring the two free corners up to meet the pinched corners.

3. Adjust the folds in the napkin to appear as in the drawing. Then lay the napkin on a flat surface and flatten it into a diamond shape. The loose corners should all be at the top of the diamond shape.

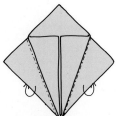

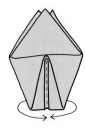

4. Folding the front layer only, bring the lower right and left folded edges inward to meet at the center.

5. Fold the remaining lower edges backward. (It is easiest to do this by turning the napkin over and repeating step 4 on the back.)

6. Fold the sharp bottom point up to touch the horizontal edges.

7. Fold the bottom of the napkin in half.

 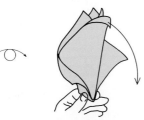  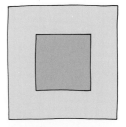

8. Hold the bottom tightly in one hand, and turn the napkin around so that the other side faces you.

9. Still holding tightly at the bottom edge, take your free hand and gently pull the front loose corner at the top away from the other loose corners. The petals of the flower will spread apart, causing your flower to "bloom."

10. Anchor the base of the flower by inserting the tines of a fork into the back of the bottom edge, or place the base into a glass.

Variation: Use two square paper napkins in different colors and different sizes, preferably 10 inches (25 cm) and 13 inches (33 cm). Center the smaller napkin over the larger napkin, then fold them together as one.

FATHER'S BIRTHDAY

FATHER'S BIRTHDAY
Necktie

Here's an appropriate design to let Dad know he's the guest of honor.

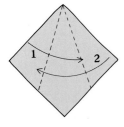

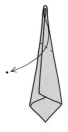

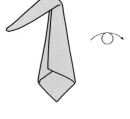

1. Begin with an open napkin with one corner pointing toward you. Divide the top corner in thirds by folding the right and left side edges that are closest to the top corner inward so that they overlap evenly.

2. Bring the long folded edges inward. They will again cross each other, dividing the thin angle into thirds.

3. Approximately one-third down the length of the napkin, fold the thin top point out to the left and slightly down, as shown in the next drawing.

4. Turn the napkin over from side to side.

5. Fold the thin point over to the left.

6. Fold the point backward, tucking it into the knot you have loosely formed.

7. Tighten and shape the knot of your finished Necktie.

FATHER'S BIRTHDAY
Shirt

This clever fold will be a sure Dad pleaser! If you are using a small napkin
(13 inches [33 cm] square or smaller), omit the first step and begin at step 2 with
a fully open napkin.

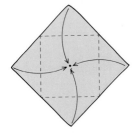

1. Begin with an open, square napkin. Fold all four corners inward to meet at the center.

2. Fold the right and left sides inward to meet at the center.

3. Fold the top edge backwards, forming a hem at the back of the top edge, approximately 1¼ inches (3 cm) wide.

4. Fold the top right and left corners inward to meet at the center gap, at a spot approximately 1¼ inches (3 cm) below the top edge. This will form the Shirt's collar.

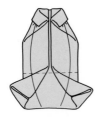

5. As you hold the collar in place with one hand, use your other hand to form the sleeves. At the bottom center of the napkin are two loose corners. Grasp each one separately and fold them outward so that they extend beyond the sides of the napkin.

6. Carefully lift the bottom edge of the napkin and fold it towards the top. Slip this edge underneath the points of the collar to lock them in place.

7. Finished Shirt.

GRANDMOTHER'S BIRTHDAY
Orchid

The beauty of this exotic flower makes it an ideal way to let Grandmother know how special she is. For the best results, fold from a napkin that is colored or patterned on both sides.

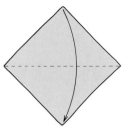

1. Begin with an open, square napkin, with one corner pointing toward you. Bring the top corner down to the bottom corner, forming a triangle.

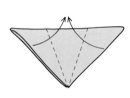

2. Fold the slanted sides inward to meet at the center.

3. Fold the long sides inward to meet at the center again.

4. Fold the bottom point up to slightly above the top of the napkin.

5. Fold the napkin in half along the vertical center.

6. Hold the bottom of the napkin to keep the last fold in place, then turn your napkin slightly to the left so that the three long points are facing you at the top of the napkin.

7. If the napkin is large, put the bottom in a glass to anchor it in place. If it is a small paper napkin, insert the tines of a fork into the bottom of the back. Pull the two side points (petals) out to the sides.

8. The center point has two layers. Pull the inner layer down.

9. Shape the petals of the finished Orchid.

GRANDFATHER'S BIRTHDAY
Bowtie

The Bowtie is smart-looking design that is quick and simple to fold.

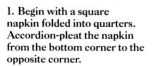

1. Begin with a square napkin folded into quarters. Accordion-pleat the napkin from the bottom corner to the opposite corner.

2. Holding the pleats tightly in one hand, slip one end through a napkin ring and slide the ring to the middle of the napkin.

3. Fan out the sides to give the napkin a Bowtie shape.

Pinwheel

Add some fun to the party table with this fanciful Pinwheel fold. Place a round candy or a small cookie at the center as an extra treat.

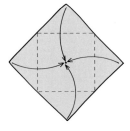

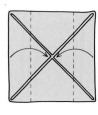

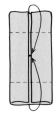

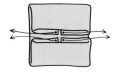

1. Begin with an open, square napkin. Fold all four corners inward to meet at the center.

2. Fold the right and left sides inward to meet at the center.

3. Fold the top and bottom edges inward to meet at the center.

4. Look under the layers where the edges meet at the center—you will see four loose corners. One at a time, pull each corner out to the side. Each corner will form a point as shown in drawing 5.

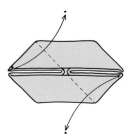

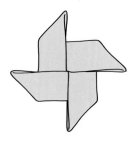

5. Fold up the top left point. Fold down the bottom right point.

6. Finished Pinwheel. If you wish, leave a straw, candy cane, licorice stick, or other fun item poking out from under a bottom edge.

CHILD'S BIRTHDAY
Clown's Hat

Send in the clowns! And set the mood for a fun-filled party with this festive fold.

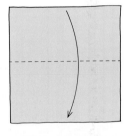

1. Begin with an open, square napkin. Bring the top edge down to the bottom edge, folding the napkin in half.

2. Bring the top right corner down to the center of the bottom edge.

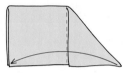

3. Bring the right point over to the bottom left corner.

4. Bring the top left corner down to the bottom right corner.

5. Separate the eight layers at the bottom of the napkin, dividing them in half—four layers in each hand. Open the napkin, shaping it into a cone.

6. Turn the open end of the cone up all around, as if turning up a cuff on a pair of pants. This will form the hat's brim.

7. Turn the pointed corner of the brim down twice, hiding it between the brim and the hat.

8. Completed Clown's Hat.

B A B Y ' S   B I R T H D A Y

Diaper

Celebrate the happy occasion of a new baby with an old-fashioned Diaper.

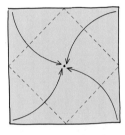

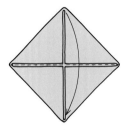

1. Begin with an open, square napkin. Bring all four corners inward to meet at the center.

2. Bring the top point down to the bottom point.

3. Curve the right and left side points inward until their tips overlap, as in drawing 4.

4. Bring the bottom point up to overlap the other two points. Secure all three points together with a safety pin.

5. Finished Diaper.

Romantic Occasions

DINNER FOR TWO
Valentine Heart

This heart shape requires a cloth or paper napkin that will take a crease well.

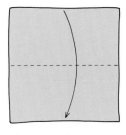

1. Begin with an open napkin. Bring the top edge down to the bottom edge, folding the napkin in half.

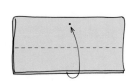

2. Bring both bottom edges up to lie approximately 1 inch (2.5 cm) below the top folded edge.

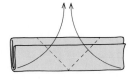

3. Put a finger at the center of the bottom edge and bring the right half of the bottom edge up to lie along the vertical center of the napkin, Repeat on the left side so that the two edges meet at the center.

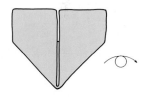

4. Turn the napkin over from side to side.

5. Fold the four corners at the top down to form small triangles as shown in the next drawing. (If you are using a cloth napkin, you may want to iron these folds in place.)

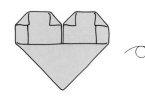

6. Turn the napkin over from side to side.

7. Finished Valentine Heart.

DINNER FOR TWO
Lover's Knot

*This design symbolizes a letter to a lover, tied securely into a knot, to be opened and
read by your love alone. Use a lightweight cloth napkin.*

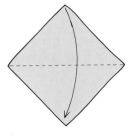

1. Begin with an open napkin.
Bring the top corner down to
the bottom corner.

2. Beginning at the bottom
corners, roll the napkin up
from bottom to top.

3. Loosely tie the roll into
a knot.

4. Completed Lover's Knot.

ANNIVERSARY
Sweetheart

This design looks particularly lovely if folded from a delicate or lacy napkin.

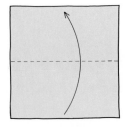 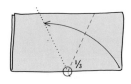  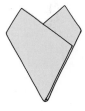

1. Begin with an open napkin. Bring the bottom edge up to the top edge, folding the napkin in half.

2. Place a finger at the center of the bottom folded edge. Bring the right half of the bottom edge up to the position shown in the next drawing.

3. Bring the remaining part of the bottom edge up to meet the slanted right edge. What was the bottom folded edge of your napkin should now be folded into thirds. Adjust your napkin so that the top points are even.

4. Finished Sweetheart.

WEDDING
Layered Heart

(Design by the author)

Reveal the secrets of your heart with this delicate design.

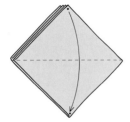

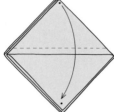

2.

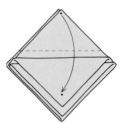

3.

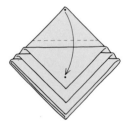

4.

1 through 4. Begin with a square napkin folded into quarters. Place it on the table so that the four free corners are at the top. Fold down each of the top corners in succession, bringing each a little higher than the previous corner.

5. You should now have all of the corners folded down and evenly spaced apart. Place a finger at the center of the top edge and fold each half of that edge down to meet at the vertical center.

6. Fold the tip of the top point backwards.

7. Lift the side flaps up and gently shape by poking the fold line up from behind.

8. Give the finished Heart a soft, curved shape.

BREAKFAST IN BED
Triple Tier

This very elegant design can also be very practical. Behind each of the three bands is a pocket for silverware, a flower, a namecard, or a secret message. Use a napkin that looks good on both sides.

1. Begin with a square napkin folded into quarters. Place the four free corners at the top of the napkin. Lift up the first free corner and roll it down as far as it will comfortably go (just past midway).

2. Flatten the band you have just formed. Lift up the second free corner and fold it backward on a line slightly above the first band. Adjust the fold to create a second band, equal in width to the first.

3. Repeat step 2 with the third layer, creating a third band slightly higher than the second and equal in width to the first two.

4. Fold the side corners backward and adjust them until they are spaced evenly apart.

5. Completed Triple Tier.

Variation: After step 3, rotate the napkin so that the remaining single corner is at the top right. Fold the right and left sides behind to form a rectangular shape with diagonal bands.

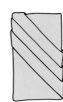

Parties

FORMAL DINNER PARTY
Double Fan

*The Double Fan is a very showy and impressive design, suitable for a formal affair.
It requires a large, stiff cotton napkin. The folding pattern is a little more difficult
than other designs, so allow yourself time to practice folding it.*

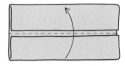

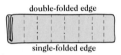

double-folded edge

single-folded edge

1. Begin with an open napkin. Fold the top and bottom edges inward to meet at the center. Then bring the bottom edge up to the top edge, folding the napkin in half.

2. Starting at one short end, accordion-pleat the napkin into eight equal parts (you will be making seven folds). Hint: If you are having trouble pleating into eighths, fold the napkin in half, then fold each half separately into quarters.

3. Hold the napkin tightly at the bottom end of the pleats. Make sure this is the end that was a single-folded edge in step 3. At the top of your napkin, each pleat is formed from a double-folded edge.

Wherever the layers bend inward to an accordion-pleat, separate the two layers by pulling the first layer forward, forming a small double-layered triangle.

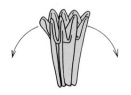

4. Repeat step 4 on all pleats that bend inward from the side at which you are looking. Still holding the napkin tightly at the bottom, turn it around from front to back.

5. Look for the pleats that bend inward on this side and repeat step 4 on all. Also fold down a small triangular flap at each end.

6. Gently allow the top points of the napkin to spread apart until the sides are resting on the table.

7. This is your completed Double Fan.

FORMAL DINNER PARTY
Wave

The spray and swirling motion of an ocean wave are reflected in this attractive and elegant design.

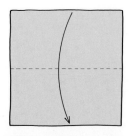

1. Begin with an open, square napkin. Bring the top edge down to the bottom edge.

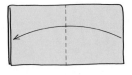

2. Bring the right side over to the left side.

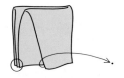

3. There are four free corners at the bottom left corner. Pick up the first corner in your right hand. As you hold the bottom three corners in place with your left hand, pull the first corner to the far right to achieve the triangular shape shown in the next drawing.

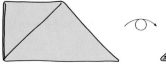

4. Carefully turn the napkin over from left to right.

5. Place a finger at the left end of the top edge. Grasp the first corner at the bottom right and gently pull it to the far left, forming a triangular shape.

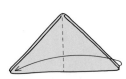

6. Fold the napkin in half from right to left.

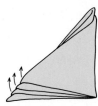

7. Slightly separate the loose points so they are evenly staggered.

8. As you hold the bottom right corner in place, softly roll the top corner backward at an angle.

9. Here is your finished Wave. If necessary, insert a fork inside the roll to weight it down and keep it from unrolling.

GARDEN PARTY
Tulip

(Design by the author)

Use this sweet and simple design to reflect your party theme.

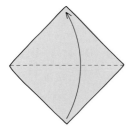

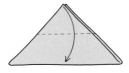

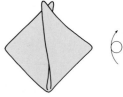

1. Begin with an open, square napkin, with one corner pointing toward you. Bring the bottom corner up to the top corner, folding the napkin into a triangle.

2. Fold the top corners down to the center of the bottom edge.

3. Fold both side points up so that they touch and slightly overlap at the top.

4. Holding the bottom sides, flip the napkin over from bottom to top.

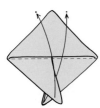

5. Fold the bottom points up so that each lies slightly to the side of the top point.

6. Fold the side points behind.

7. Finished Tulip.

TEA PARTY

Lazy Susan

(Design by the author)

This clever design divides into five compartments to conveniently hold table fare at your next party. Use it to hold finger foods, snacks, candy, tea bags, or sugar packets.

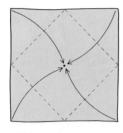 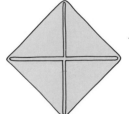 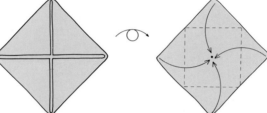 

1. Begin with an open, square napkin. The patterned, or better, side of the napkin should be facing up. Fold all four corners inward to meet at the center.

2. Holding the center corners securely in place, carefully turn the napkin over.

3. Fold the four outside corners inward to meet at the center.

4. Again, fold the four outside corners inward to meet at the center.

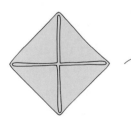 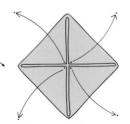 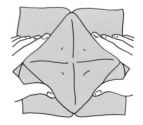 

5. Holding the center corners securely in place, carefully turn the napkin over.

6. Unfold each of the four triangular flaps, bringing each corner from the center outward.

7. Insert a finger at the edge of each of the four pockets. Gently push your fingers together, forming the center square into a 3-dimensional star shape.

8. Place the completed Lazy Susan into a bowl to hold its 3-dimensional shape.

CHILDREN'S PARTY
Cat's Ears

This fun fold can be placed on the table already opened, or fold it up through step 3 and then show your guests how to pull the corners apart to make and wear their own Cat's Ears.

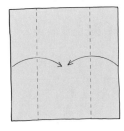

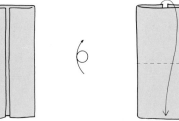

1. Begin with an open, cloth napkin. Fold the sides in to meet at the center.

2. Turn the napkin over.

3. Fold the top edges down to the bottom.

4. At the center of the bottom edge, find two loose corners. Then peek under the napkin to find two more loose corners. Grasp the two right loose corners (upper and lower) in your right hand. Grasp the two left loose corners (upper and lower) in your left hand. Be sure you are holding only the corners and not the edges in between them, then pull your hands apart.

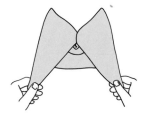

5. Flip the napkin over your head so that the two points are now sticking up…

6. …and show off your pair of feline ears!

CHILDREN'S PARTY
Surprise Sack

The fun part of this fold is finding little goodies to put inside. Try candy, small toys,
a noisemaker, a fortune, or a clue for a treasure hunt!

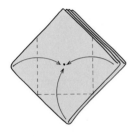   

1. Begin with a square napkin folded into quarters. Place the four free corners at the top. Fold the bottom and side corners inward to meet at the center.

2. Holding the flaps in place, turn the napkin over from side to side.

3. Fold down the first two layers of the top corner.

4. Completed Surprise Sack. Tuck a surprise into the pocket.

Picture Index

This index will help you select the best napkin fold for any occasion. Just choose the design you want by looking at the finished result here, then turn to the corresponding page for folding instructions.

Basket
24

Bowtie
92

Buffet Brunch Bundle
16

Bunny
18

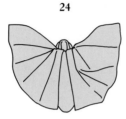

Butterfly
50

Candle
32

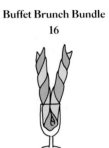

Candy Cane
44

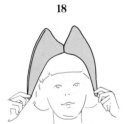

Cat's Ears
122

Christmas Tree
40

Clown's Hat
96

Cocktail Coaster
14

Corsage
83

Diaper
98

Double Fan
114

Double Leaf
66

Elf's Boot
37

Fireside Flame
70

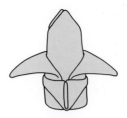

Fleur-de-Lis
21

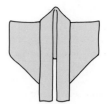

Happi Coat
68

Ice Cream Cone
62

Icicle
72

Layered Heart
108

Lazy Susan
120

Lover's Knot
104

Necktie
86

Orchid
90

Parasol
52

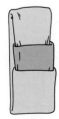

Picnic Package
64

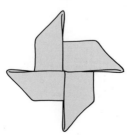

Pinwheel
94

Rose
80

Santa Claus
34

Shell
60

Shirt
88

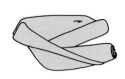

Sleigh
76

Snowflake
74

Standing Christmas Tree
42

Star of David
29

Stocking
46

Surprise Sack
124

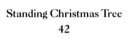

Sweetheart
106

Triple Tier
110

Tulip
118

Twin Baskets
26

Valentine Heart
102

Water Lily
54

Wave
116

Yacht
57